To Grow My Garden Within

A Spiritual Memoir: Cultivating the Journey

Dr. Gloria J. Hill

Author of *The Nature Whisperer: Seasons of Light*

ISBN 978-1-63814-469-4 (Paperback)
ISBN 978-1-63814-470-0 (Digital)

Covenant Books
11661 Hwy 707
Murrells Inlet, SC 29576
www.covenantbooks.com

Dedicated to the flowers in my garden: My darling
daughter Lauren, Lucas, Marco and Lianna,
and to Don who keeps me grounded.

TO GROW MY GARDEN WITHIN

Clippers and snippers
My garden tools,
Those gnarly and tangled knots.
How tight their hold
With roots so bold,
Their fierce and mighty cling.
When all I need is
The faith of a mustard seed,
To grow my garden within.

Perennials

*What lies behind us and what lies ahead are tiny
matters compared to what is seeded within.*
—Henry David Thoreau

MESSAGE IN THE WINDOW

A mother's love knows no bounds. Her spirit transcends earthly dimensions, revealed in the light.

Connie was cleaning her mother's house for the last time. It was the kind of cleaning that is an undoing, a numbing removal of a life lived. Since that fateful day, grief was Connie's constant companion. Now her life was divided into two periods: the time before and the time after Mom died.

In the time before, she and her mother had plans. They would visit gardens and art festivals and do some antiquing in scenic towns, the places that time had forgotten. After Connie's retirement, they would have all the time in the world to leisurely explore quaint little hamlets.

But time was not on their side.

A call came from the hospital; it changed everything. Even the ringtone sounded urgent. It started a course of events that ran away from reality. The voice on the phone said, "Come to the hospital. Quick." Her mom might not survive the night.

It was as though her mother was waiting for her. Connie arrived in time to sit with her, holding her hand until her mother drew her last breath. Then began the time after, when Connie's own heartbeat drummed hollow inside her, each *lub-dub* echoing a strange alternate universe, a life without her mother. The planned outings that would never be faded into an unreachable fog. She wondered if a person could die from so much heartbreak, so much loss.

A heavy numbness invaded Connie's life over the next few weeks. Condolences from family and friends offered loving support, somewhat dulling the pain. But grief is a stranglehold that wraps around you, choking your life. It bookends your days with a stabbing reminder each morning and a heavy tired heart at night.

Then came the chore of her clearing out her mom's apartment.

It took two weekends. Connie was about to take her last step out the door. Lugging the last few forgotten items, she turned around for one last look. With tear-filled eyes, she surveyed the bare rooms in the hollowed-out house. Her eyes settled on a nondescript window with old lace curtains still hanging. Just then a slight breeze floated into the room, and the curtain waved a bit, as if to punctuate her final departure with a soft goodbye.

A Cradled Heart

Throughout the ordeal, Connie felt a loving essence that sustained her, a presence that seemed to cradle her aching heart. And now, that loving spirit gave her a little nudge. It took the form of a sudden and unexplained urge to put everything down, take out her cell phone, and take a picture of that lacey-curtained window. A click later and that window was preserved in a photo and, just as quickly, forgotten.

Discovery

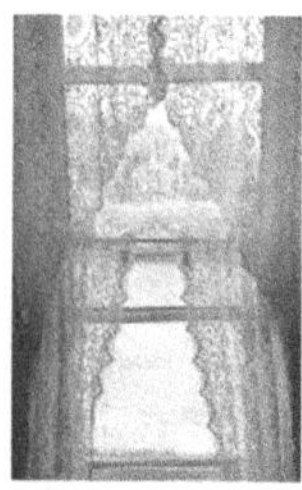

Connie was looking for a way out of her grief. Call it a sign or something, anything that would let her know her mom was in a good place. She did not know she already had it. While sharing photos with a friend, the picture of the window slid into view. To Connie it was still just a photo of a window, but her friend said to her, "Look again, Connie."

She looked. Utterly surprised, she blurted out, "How did I not see that?"

There, in plain sight, was an arrow pointing upward. It was green and radiated light. It signaled to her like a gateway, a portal. And that was when grief loosened its tight grip and set her soul free. Aloud she whispered, "Thank you, Mom."

Windows: Continuity of Life

Connie's story compelled me to think more about spiritual symbols, colors, and their meanings. Colors are mentioned in the Old and New Testaments hundreds of times. I also looked to artists as well as writers. I discovered that green is the universal color of new life, rebirth, and immortality. Then I found a commonality regarding windows as a metaphor. A window is a threshold for new perspectives. It invites the soul to move freely, breaking down boundaries. The upward arrow signifies continuity.

I thought about the beautiful stained-glass windows adorning the small church in my hometown. Each one was a beautiful work of art, yet I was always drawn to one window—the one I sat by every Sunday, the one that was kept open.

THE COURAGE TO LOVE AGAIN

Imprinting: If separated, swans will mourn the loss and return to familiar areas.

A pair of trumpeter swans return to my pond each spring. I dubbed them Mr. Darcy and Ms. Bennet. I wondered if they, like their Jane Austen counterparts, faced challenges in their courtship. So I began to research swan behaviors. I learned that swans imprint on a mate and an area, forming a strong bond to ward off would-be predators. If separated they will return to familiar areas to find each other. As they face dangers along the way, the urge to reunite is strong. They mate for life. If one partner dies, the other will mourn for months before looking for another mate. It sounds like a Hallmark romance, the stuff of Hollywood, and not too far from home.

I often see this lady sitting on a bench near the pond, her yellow straw hat catching my attention. I wonder about her. Why is she alone? Was she always alone? Why this place?

One morning, I stopped to say a brief hello. She offered her hand, her name, and her story.

Kathleen chooses this bench to sit and watch geese and other waterfowl glide over the pond's surface. This bench is particularly meaningful. Her back presses against a brass plate that has an inscription. It is a dedication to her late husband, Jim.

In his lifetime, Jim was an ardent protector of natural wildlife. Together they would sit there to watch herons, egrets, and swans flourish in their own habitat. After more than fifty years of marriage, life without Jim is challenging. Author Barbara Kingsolver, in her bestselling novel *Unsheltered*, observed that loss of a loved one does not occur in one day. Loss happens each day for those who keep living. To soften the loss, Kathleen returns to this bench where she first thanks God for the beauty of the day, followed by her "chat" with Jim. It is here by the pond, on this bench, that she returns to find her mate.

Imprinting: Rapid learning, usually happening at birth, establishes long-lasting behavioral responses to a place or living thing.

Homing Instinct

Do humans have a homing instinct? Researchers cannot say for sure, but neither can they rule it out. My story might be convincing evidence though. Fourteen years ago, I felt an undeniable yearn to go home. I was three thousand miles away. In that same year, Michael Bublé's song "Home" became a number one hit and went platinum. Apparently, I was not the only one longing for home.

After forty years living in the West, first Colorado and then California, I began to think of my growing-up years in Southern New Jersey. Forgotten places—like the thickly wooded Pine Barrens, briny backwater lagoons, the Atlantic shore, and acres of farmlands— now took up primary spaces in my heart. Likewise, coupled with my mounting nostalgia toward home was an increasing detachment from my current life. I began to question my life choices. Then came the unmistakable tug. Whatever kept me loosely tethered to my East Coast roots now felt like a fully extended bungee cord ripping me back, with urgency. And somehow, I knew it was God's hand pulling me home.

> For I know the thoughts that I think toward
> you, saith the LORD, thoughts of peace, and not
> of evil, to give you an expected end. (Jer. 29:11
> KJV)

It was the worst time to relocate. In 2006, markets were falling and houses devalued, yet I put my faith in the hand that drew me home. There was a financial cost to this move, yet my emotional income was sky-high. There were rainbows upon rainbows. My daughter met the love of her life, a man from my hometown who was to become her husband and father of my three grandchildren. I returned to find my circle of family and friends intact, as though I never left. And, while my peers were planning their retirements, I began a whole new career. It was the stuff of my dreams, becoming a professor of education at my alma mater, Rowan University. Full circle, indeed. But there was more. Unexpectedly, when I was not looking, I fell in love, again.

After divorce, I spent seven years living alone, loving my solitude. My everyday life was calm and peaceful. I felt free from the tedium of relationship building. I told friends I was liberated from the constant, never-ending negotiation of everything. All decisions were my own. No debates. No battles. No recriminations when expectations were not met. I was living in my head, my heart fully protected behind strong walls. I constructed these walls, brick upon brick, with mortar from hardened tears—a wall that sealed off any intent to love again. But God had other plans.

Paired Swans Form Strong Lifelong Bonds

Don was my best "guy friend" in college. We had many classes together, astronomy being a favorite. Our professor held evening outdoor classes, affectionately dubbed "star parties," where we paired off cuddling together to keep warm while identifying constellations in the wintry night sky. By day there were afternoon walks and idle chats. Along with others in our circle of friends, we often met for lunch.

I recall that sunny afternoon when he asked me to the prom. We were walking together after class. It was one of those spectacularly crisp October afternoons, when the sun flashed through tall oak trees and red and gold leaves drifted slowly to the ground. It was the kind of day when everything feels wondrously in order. As Don pivoted left to enter the student union building, he stopped abruptly and then turned and asked, "Hey, Glor, want to go to the prom with me?"

Like the falling autumn leaves, going to the prom with Don felt like the most natural thing in the world.

"Sure," I answered without hesitation.

The next two summers following graduation brought fewer and fewer get-togethers. Soon life pulled us in different directions. I sprinted toward new adventures in the West. Don remained in Southern New Jersey. We lost track of each other. The years ticked by.

If Separated, Bonded Swans Will Return to Familiar Places to Reunite

Four decades later, fueled by faith, my daughter and I returned to New Jersey. A reunion celebrating my return brought the old college gang together again. We gathered at my new condo. I will never forget the moment Don walked up my driveway. My heart did flip-flops, and I could not breathe. The sparks seemed to fly out through my fingertips. It was electric but not shocking. There was a knowing.

We talked all evening. Then the daily, even hourly, emails flew back and forth. How did we miss all those cues so long ago? Each photo from our college years showed us standing together, shoulder to shoulder.

Reconnecting with Don felt as normal as the rising sun. Forty years after our first date (the prom), we had our second date. My nomadic heart was beginning to feel grounded. My wall of autonomy was eroding. But it did not dissolve entirely. Even with the crumbling of my fortress, it was not easy for me to allow someone into my orderly life. And what about Don? Did he have challenges of his own to conquer?

There is the lightness of loving, and then there is the heavy downbeat of living. I doubt if Mr. Darcy and Ms. Bennet had to negotiate a division of labor. I wondered, *Can two histories, formed three thousand miles apart, live harmoniously and find their side-by-side groove?* A second-time-around romance, even when you are lucky enough to fall in love with your best friend, is not always easy.

Cracks to Let in God's Light

I heard that God gives us cracks so that his light can shine through. There were fissures.

In this new love, I occasionally felt I was in over my head. The old urge to retreat to my fortress returned. I still believed in God's plan for us, but we needed help. Going out again on faith, there came a time when I asked Don to kneel with me to pray. A bit off-balance and hesitant about what to say, we knelt. It was not an eloquent prayer but an earnest plea asking for help, petitioning God's light to shine new insight through the holes in this relationship. Then we pledged a commitment to find the courage to face issues, to do the hard work of listening and finding resolutions. The bond we forged so long ago was strengthening. We made time to discuss, to have those courageous conversations, and to understand each other. Hard work has its perks. We danced.

Adult swans, crowned with pure white feathers, begin a courtship that resembles a dance, a ruffling of feathers. They touch beaks to kiss, their necks forming a heart.

Don and I are snowbirds. Crowned in thinning locks of gray and white, we seniors flock together to the town squares. Like our kindred swans, we migrate hundreds of miles south each winter, where we gather with fellow retirees, in a playground for seniors. Every day is a weekend. We flourish here, frequenting the town squares any night of the week to hear live bands playing the oldies. We hop in our golf carts, tootling alongside cotton candy sunsets, to dance under the stars.

> For where two or three are gathered together
> in my name, there am I in the midst of them.
> (Matt. 18:20)

Love is not for the faint of heart. It requires courage. I think of the courageous conversations that I should have had with others, so long ago. Tangled up in emotional knots and too proud or too stubborn to ask for God's help, I missed opportunities. But once bonded, I believe it is never too late to be reunited, even in spirit.

I think of Kathleen sitting by the pond. There are benches waiting for us, places to reunite with loved ones. Like Kathleen and Jim, we can sit and chat. It is never too late. I imagine Kathleen telling Jim things she neglected to say in years past.

High above I see Canada geese in their V formation, heading homeward. Home is where we relish in the power to renew. Love is the renewable energy that powers the universe.

Wounds of the heart need light…not armor.

OCTOBER'S BLUE MOON

I am so glad I live in a world where there are Octobers.
            —L. M. Montgomery

Me too, Anne. I love Octobers. And this one is incredibly special. October 2020 arrived with bonanza of lunar events: a harvest moon (full moon closest to the autumnal equinox), a hunter's moon (follows the harvest moon), and a blue moon, happening on the thirty-first, Halloween. And Don and I were able to share it with Lily, our new friend.

After a light supper and still distancing in the era of COVID, we walked our new neighbor home. Even though it was a short walk, we did not get far before we stopped in our tracks. And there it was, fresh and clean, looking like a prop in a movie set, the kind of moon George Bailey would lasso for his Mary. We stopped to drink in its delicious glow, the perfect aperitif to a lovely evening.

We swallowed it up.

The Mistress of the Night

Henry David Thoreau dubbed the full moon as the mistress of the night. She reminds us of who we are without the tight knots. We drop all pretenses. Grinding noises rambling in our brains cease to exist. The years fade away. Bathed in buoyant reverie, we return to our bloom, where love floats up from places we thought were lost. On these special nights, when we are lucky enough to be held in her wondrous spell, our mistress of the night dazzles while she silently waves her wand over the tidal ebbs. Our hearts fill with oceans of love. We are moonstruck.

Allow me to wax romantic. We all have a love story or two in our hearts. Make a little space for Judy and Jim. This is their story.

To Dance in the Moonlight, One Last Time: Jim and Judy's Story

To some, much is given; to others, much is asked. Jim would place himself as the former. But it is also true that life had asked much of Jim. In the 1960s at age twenty-two, Jim was exposed to Agent Orange while serving his country in Vietnam. There were early signs of physical distress. And twenty years later, with progressing symptoms, the diagnosis came: Parkinson's disease. Then began the steady decline.

Jim was an outdoorsman. He loved biking, cross-country skiing, and softball. But Parkinson's is a thief that steals life one day at a time. Little by little, the physical activities he loved were becoming too challenging. But Jim kept trying, with painful results. Eventually, the time came when he could not stand up on his own. It takes courage to face a progressive deteriorating disease. During the last eighteen months of his life, he was confined to a wheelchair in an assisted living facility. He continued to be grateful for his loving wife and family. To him, much was given. He had Judy.

Forty-Nine Roses

They met in college. While leaving a class on a bright sunny autumn day, Judy noticed him laughing and joking with a group of friends. Inwardly she mused, *How can I meet someone like him?*

She felt drawn to his easy laughter, his positive sway with friends. For several days, she would look for him after class, but always from a distance. Her shyness kept her from approaching him. But fate brought them together at a college mixer. One date led to another and another. They fell in love and married right after Jim returned from Vietnam. Jim knew how lucky he was to have found his soul mate. They celebrated their life together. For the next forty-nine years, Jim gave Judy a single rose on Valentine's Day.

May I Have This Dance?

It was Valentine's Day, a beautiful evening. The assisted care facility where Jim was now a resident organized a dance. Tables were decorated with red hearts and white lace. A wall of floor-to-ceiling windows brought the outside world into view. A tired sun was sinking, leaving behind flattened layers of pinks and purples, pancaked between a few wispy clouds, the remnants of the day. And toward the east, a full moon was beginning its ordained path across the starry heavens, sweeping across a dreamy heart or two.

Looking very smart in her new red outfit, Judy arrived early to spend a few quiet moments with Jim before the others arrived. And waiting for her was her Jim with a single rose to celebrate forty-nine years of marriage. They kissed and talked softly, held in the magic of moonlight and soft music.

As the room filled with other couples and their families, Judy went to get some refreshments for the two of them. While she was gone, Jim had a melancholy look about him. It caught the attention of Janis, a frequent volunteer who often attended events at the residence. She knew this was rare for Jim who was such an upbeat guy. Some couples were already on the dance floor, gliding to timeless love songs. Jim watched longingly. Sensing Jim's pensive mood and feeling something was awry, Janis sat down with him and asked him if he needed some assistance.

Looking wistfully away and feeling the pull of the moon, he simply said, "It's Valentine's Day. I would just love to dance with my wife."

Janis looked about the room, seeing the couples dancing. She looked up at the full moon now higher in the night sky, and a wave of an idea rippled through her mind. Tilting her head to one side and smiling, she turned to Jim and said, "Maybe you can."

The Dance Sandwich

By the time Judy returned to the table with a tray of goodies, Janis and Jim were beaming almost as brightly as the moon. She walked over to Jim with questioning eyes.

"What are you two scheming?"

That was when Janis walked over and stood in front of Jim, guiding him off his wheelchair to a standing position. Then she maneuvered around holding him up from behind, giving Jim the opportunity to ask his wife a question. His broad smile freed him from his fragile body long enough to ask, "May I have this dance?"

Beaming, Judy began to dance with her upright husband with Janis holding him up from behind. Together, the three of them made a dance sandwich.

Call it kismet, but at that moment, an introduction to a familiar song began to play. It was Anne Murray singing: "Could I have this dance?"

I would surmise that when Jim laid his head on his pillow that night, remembering how it felt to hold his Judy in his arms once more, the words "When we're together, it feels so right" probably lulled him into a deep sleep. It was a night of which dreams are made. To him, much had been given.

October paints us a canvas of life cycles. American naturalist John Burroughs wrote, "How beautifully leaves grow old. How full of light and color are their last days."

Jim and Judy did not make it to their fiftieth wedding anniversary. I know, you do not want a sad ending here. But endings and beginnings have no space between them. They are the same. Jim began his new beginning. He will welcome his love in her new beginning, in the fullness of time.

> Love is our true destiny. We do not find the
> meaning of life by ourselves alone—we find it
> with another. (Thomas Merton, *Love and Living*)

And when I looked, the moon had turned to gold.

ONE DISH AT A TIME

I had a question. Well, I had many questions. My younger self contemplated thoughts too big for my little mind. I would save them up. Then, when I could be confident of securing my mother's full attention, they would spill out.

My favorite platform for my deepest questions was in the kitchen when we did the dishes. She washed, and I dried. I would usually begin with an attention-grabber that would lead to my bigger, more pressing questions.

"Mom," I announced, "I feel sorry for God."

"What on earth for?" she returned, a bit stunned by my statement.

"Because there are too many people for God to love and some of them are not nice."

"Well," she started, "God can do anything, even loving everyone at once, no matter who they are and what they do. He loves them anyway, sending his angels to help them be better people, better daughters, better sons, better parents, and better neighbors."

And that response led me to finally ask the bigger question, the one weighing heavily on my soul.

"But I am supposed to love my neighbor as myself. At church I learned that everyone is my neighbor. How can *I* love so many people at one time?"

My mom heaved a big sigh and took some time before she answered. "Well, when it gets hard, think of it as the way we do the dishes—one dish at a time."

Journeys

The miles I have traveled
For mysteries unraveled.
Often lost and scattered
To find what matters.

Wings made for flight,
And a compass of light,
Over land and sea-foam,
Not flying alone.

My soul in formation
With no hesitation.
I will take that journey,
Again and again.

THE BRIDGE THAT CARRIES US OVER

Out of the blue, I decided to build a small ornamental footbridge for my garden. I thought my grandchildren would enjoy the shortcut to the pond. That is what I told myself.

I purchased a kit. According to the reviews, it would take three hours to assemble. It took me four days.

No matter. I had the time. It was May in the time of COVID. Having just returned from Florida, I was in a two-week quarantine. Distanced from everything and everybody, the walls began to close in on me. This project helped to fill the time.

As the bridge began to take shape, I also began to feel an elevated kind of liberation. My spirits lifted. More than a charming ornament for the garden, my bridge offered me a sense of connections. It carried me across a self-imposed threshold. And when I thought more about it, I realized the deeper meaning and the lure of bridges.

Connections, Allure, and Discoveries

Many of us have a fascination with bridges. Living and playing along the eastern seaboard, I recognize an acute rise of my senses when driving over the bridges that arc over rivers and bays. I love the old Walt Whitman Bridge that spans the Delaware River, connecting New Jersey with Pennsylvania. Less grand but nonetheless compelling is the small bridge only 1500 feet from my home. Instinctively, when driving across the narrow gauge, I look out my car window to the small inlet that flows to the bay. My mind drifts out to the beyond. With no limitations, I sail into the realm of possibilities.

On the Brink of Everything

In his book *On the Brink of Everything*, Parker Palmer creates a powerful mix of expectation and unbounded hope. Maybe that is why I moved my writing table to the back of the house, in full view of my small footbridge. It symbolized my entryway to everything.

My young grandchildren live their lives on the brink of everything. Learning is their life's work. They stumble. They get up. They try new ways. They fail. They keep reaching beyond their grasp. Undeterred, they live on the threshold of unbounded hope.

TRUST: A DISTANT VOICE

It was years ago, and although time has softened the wounds, I can easily retrieve the emotional upheaval. Divorce is a wretched undoing. An emotional earthquake. It shapeshifts your inner tectonic plates, the aftershocks of which continue for years. Reeling from loss of solid ground, loss of identity, tired, depressed, I slow-walked my life. I was devoid of emotion. Dark clouds hid the sunshine in my daughter's face.

Drowning in pain, I also lost something I could not name. I was on a runaway train, taking me to an unknown frightening world. I could not hear my own heartbeat. A distant voice I used to know tried to reach me. I strained to hear it.

"You will find it again. Trust."

I wanted to believe in that voice, but I had no strength to go the distance and even doubted its existence. But that barely audible sound was patiently persistent.

"Trust in *me*."

I wanted to trust in that voice. In a desperate attempt to cling to its simple message, I grabbed a permanent black marker, and I wrote on a 3 × 5 note card: TRUST. Emboldened. Two inches tall. All caps.

Trust in what or whom? I did not know. I had forgotten. Fixating on this one thought, I kept this card with me, close to my body, folded in my pocket. My TRUST card became my talisman. When fears grabbed my throat, threatening my very breath, I would take the card out and look at it. I began to think of the two large Ts as scaffolds holding me up.

TrusT

And thus began my journey to reclaim that loving voice, a voice that beat stronger and more familiar as I began to heal.

> Trust in the LORD with all your heart and
> lean not on your own understanding; in all your
> ways submit to him, and he will make your paths
> straight. (Prov. 3:5–6)

I would like to say that from that point on, I had no need for my TrusT card. But life presents many crossroads. Which path to take? Whose voice is in your ear?

Forgive the twenty-first-century tech analogy, but just as I easily click a link to track a package, I mentally "click" my TrusT card to track my life's path. It is my directional vane, redirecting me to the one consistent voice that will never abandon me. It never has. It never will. The good shepherd will leave his flock to find the one sheep. I was found.

> What man of you, having a hundred sheep,
> if he lose one of them, doth not leave the ninety
> and nine in the wilderness, and go after that
> which is lost, until he find it? (Luke 15:4)

Tucked in a breeze
Is salt from the seas,
Sway from trees,
And a touch that eases
The mind.
Slow down your pace
As it brushes your face.
It comes with traces
Of knowings
To find.

Forgiving Yourself

> There are four things you cannot take back:
> the spoken word, a spent arrow, neglected oppor-
> tunities, and the past. (Native American folklore)

I would like the luxury of going back for a redo of my past. There are words I would like to take back. On occasion, I have allowed pivotal opportunities to slip away, words that should have been spoken and were kept silent. While I have not shot any arrows, it pains me to know that some of my insensitive words have pierced skin and drew blood.

I have sought and received forgiveness from those I hurt. I have felt the healing power of God's grace. And I have forgiven myself hundreds of times, hoping the last one will stick. But something else lingers on—maybe guilt or regret. Am I not fully embracing the gift of grace, or is that just another failure?

Isn't it natural to regret mistakes?

More questions emerge. Is regret just part of the ashes that remain after forgiveness? Is there a second and third act after remorse? What am I missing? I seem to be harboring a propensity for self-imposed penance, even after forgiveness, rehashing my most devastating mistakes. They can replay over and over, like a psychological earworm, laden with harsh self-admonishments.

How could I? Why didn't I? Why didn't I know better?

Centuries ago, religious extremists would flog themselves bloody with barbed whips, to atone for their sins. We see this repugnant behavior as barbaric, yet we humans often weaponize our shortcomings, taking a switch to our emotional psyches. Some call it "beating yourself up." I do not believe that God wants us to be self-defeating. We were made for a higher purpose.

A Path toward Healing

My spirit was on a path, searching for an escape valve, a way to release me from a self-imposed emotional bondage. And there it was—the way forward. A door opened, and I experienced a world of unburdened whimsy, adorned with grace.

We were spending a few days with friends in beautiful Sarasota, Florida. They suggested a visit to the Marietta Museum of Art and Whimsy. Hmmm. Intriguing name. A short drive later, we were strolling into lush gardens dotted with fanciful art and playful sculptures, some hanging from tree limbs and others intermeshed with crawling vines. Sunlight flickered through bushy foxtail palms, dancing and tickling over blue cows, pink dragons, and red monkeys.

Ribbons of curvy, thick branches, radiating from massive tree trunks, ran throughout the gardens. They undulated up and down and over purple tigers and shimmering butterflies. Tilting my head in varied angles, I felt propelled by a vibrant force of quirky colors and playful abandon. Energy shot out my outstretched arms like electric stars. I felt as though I swallowed up the sun. My spirit twirled me round and round. I imagined myself doing the Julie Andrews spin on top of the Bavarian Alps. My brain tried desperately to hold on to the ride.

This was a pivotal experience for me. Certainly, I had enjoyed beautiful gardens and childlike fantasies before, but this was different. A rearrangement.

Rearrangement of Thought: Fusing Grace, Light, and Creation

My brain erupted into an avalanche of thoughts. Let there be light. The Shema, a prayer that celebrates creation. And 2 Timothy that speaks of grace given to us before the beginning of time.

Spectacular images of exploding electrons raced through my mind. And right there, in all this commotion of my senses, the words *grace*, *light*, and *creation* fused together and became inseparable. Time evaporated. And I was feeling creation, not as "one and done" event but as an ongoing, spontaneous emergence of light. And in that light, created for me, was boundless grace. Grace is ongoing, and my story is ongoing. In that whimsical garden, where yellow mushrooms sprouted like moonbeams and colors twirled me around like a child's spinning top, I found my own rebirth, my own big bang.

Show Up for Your Own Recreation Story

When the full spectrum of grace is revealed, there is no room for regrets.

Consider Peter, one of Jesus's early disciples. Following the arrest of Jesus, Peter denied knowing Jesus three times. Imagine the remorse he carried, the three denials that he could not take back. But Peter's failures were not the end of his story. He chose to be present in his own rebirth, his own creation story. He became the rock, upon which Jesus would build his church.

What about my story? Still wondering about the threads that weave whimsy, light, and grace together, I searched for additional insights. I was not a lone voice in this quest. My search found poets, musicians, photographers, artists, and writers who channel grace and whimsy.

Bob Goff, author of *Love Does: Discover a Secretly Incredible Life in an Ordinary World*, wrote, "Whimsy doesn't care if you are the driver or the passenger; all that matters is that you are on your way. You don't need a plan; you just need to be present."[1]

I also found whimsy closer to home. I have a friend who does whimsy better than anyone else I know. Sandy knows something about imagination that I am just beginning to understand. Her home is sprinkled with fanciful art. And anyone who visits catches her spirit, like a breeze in a flowing windsock.

And to punctuate these thoughts on rebirth, my eyes settle on a large cluster of vivid green leaves climbing along the many branches of my live oak in my own backyard. These vines were not there yesterday. Resurrection fern typically looks shriveled and dormant, hardly noticeable. But within twenty-four hours of a rainfall, it rebounds into a vibrant, leafy plant, covering the branches with lush green life.

I fail. I have failed. I will fail.

There. I have conjugated the present, past, and future of my human condition. But my story is ongoing, and so is yours. The

---

[1] Bob Goff, *Love Does: Discover a Secretly Incredible Life in an Ordinary World* (Nashville: Thomas Nelson, 2012)

important thing is to not miss the next act of your own story. Plan to show up…as a participant in your own creation story…

…and to twirl.

He hath saved us and called us with a holy calling, not according to our works, but according to his own purpose and grace, which was given to us in Christ Jesus before time began. (2 Tim. 1:9)

The Fruit of the Vine

Happiness is a vine that takes root,
and grows within the heart,
never outside it.
—Khalil Gibran

CAPACITY: TO STRETCH,
TO FEEL, TO GROW

Note: Capacity was tested in the era of COVID. Every day the bravery of our first responders leaps off the pages of our newspapers. Can we truly grasp the magnitude of their daily sacrifice?

They lose patients, their colleagues, and they worry about infecting their own families. Yet, with full weight of life itself on their sagging shoulders, they return to heal and even to grieve, just one more time. Inhaling the stench of loss, they exhale *resolve*. Then with a new lungful of air, they show up again, putting everything on the line. With angel wings at their feet, they essentially say, "I will be the one who shows up to save, to heal, and sometimes to say goodbye." With so much suffering, are we losing the capacity to feel?

These days I am reminded of the tangled jack pine and its rejuvenating power packed into hard-shelled cones. I think about it because we are weary and in need of renewal.

Capacity: Lessons from Nature

Living in beautiful Lake Arrowhead was like living in an enchanted forest, the stuff of fairy-tale stories. Perched high in the San Bernardino Mountains of Southern California, our mile-high life was cradled in natural beauty. Picturesque mountain lakes lapped gently on quiet shores, tickling the feet of the majestic redwoods. Sugar pines reached so high they seemed to touch the heavens. And far from city noise and lights, trillions and trillions of glittering stars salted the dark night sky.

Snuggled tightly alongside hundreds of trees was our little mountain home. While we slept, we often heard the splashing of raccoons, our nocturnal visitors, romping in the basin of our outdoor fountain. Squawking blue jays owned the airways, their complaints bouncing off the rocks and trees. Amid the natural beauty, there was one curious tree at the top of our driveway that gave me pause. The tree looked more like a weed than its cousins, the tall pines. I considered yanking it out from the rocks from which it sprang, and then I learned something important about this tree.

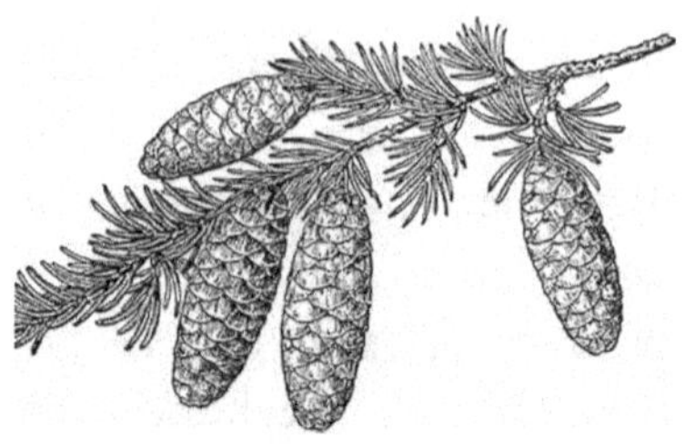

It was a jack pine, scraggly and irregular in shape, also known as a serotinous tree. Its pinecones hold a tightly bound life force that is only released during extreme heat. I thought how remarkable of nature, of God, to build in a release valve, a mechanism that houses the capacity to regenerate.

So I wonder about my own capacity for compassion. Am I too compressed to feel? Do I look away? Do I marginalize the loss? Do I cast blame, or do I call on my own first responder, the loving infinite healing spirit of God?

To Stretch, to Feel, to Grow: *One More Time*

Like the serotinous pine cones, I believe we house a great potential to love, to heal, and to renew. How much potential? I am not sure. But this I know: while I may not have unlimited capacity, with help from God and my angels, I can care, I can feel compassion, and I can respond in prayer, always one more time.

The LORD is my strength and song and is
become my salvation. (Ps. 118:14)

SEAWEED

An excellent source of vitamin A, for better
eyesight, traveling in blue-gray channels from the
microscopic to large underwater kelp forests.

"Sea" What Can Be

How clever the sea,
The way she teases me,
Rushing secrets to shore
And me wanting more…

Tireless and restless,
Rolling hypnotic rhythm.
We watch and listen
For more…

Lying here on the shore
Is a golden pearl,
Shining and twilit
And born from grit.

Jewels from oceans'
Continual motion
Say,
"Regenerate with me
And 'sea' what can be."

THE SECOND LIGHT RULE

Abundance is not in the gathering. Abundance is in the seeing.
—G. Hill

Hurricane Isaias

Earlier this month, Hurricane Isaias hammered the East Coast with rain and heavy winds. Given advance warnings, we prepared. We stocked up on food, and we armed our homes with an array of backup light. Yet, even with the best intentions of readiness, it was still a shock when electrical power was lost.

All went dark. Stone quiet. TV blinked off, clocks ceased to tick, and refrigerators stopped their humming. Stunned, I sat in the crush of abject stillness.

Heard but Unheard, Seen but Unseen

I wondered if sight is like sound in that respect. We can arrive after driving to a destination without any recollection of how we got there. We muse in wonderment, *I don't recall making those turns.* Researchers have a name for this: situational blindness. It is a failure to see what is in plain sight. In the silence of Hurricane Isaias, this question emerged: What am I seeing but not seeing?

Prophet of Light

While the storm raged outside, I settled into a sheltered reprieve where candlelight danced on the wall. I studied the interplay between light and dark. Senses became acute, more alert. And they echoed me inward, illuminating forgotten inner spaces. Then I thought of Isaiah, not the hurricane of similar name but the prophet who foretold of the light to come if only we had eyes to see.

Arise, shine, for your light has come, and
the glory of the LORD rises upon you. (Isa. 60:1)

A Time to See

Before his conversion on the road to Damascus, Saul was spiritually blind, seeing but not seeing. Blinded by self-righteousness and a raging adrenaline to hunt down the troublemakers who followed Jesus, he was overtaken by an abundance of light. When he opened his eyes, he saw for the first time, and Paul was transformed. With almost two hundred references, the theme of light is threaded throughout the Bible.

So is blindness.

We learn from the gospels that the disciples did not completely grasp Jesus's parables and teachings. They heard, but they did not hear. They saw but did not see. In Matthew 15:16, Jesus asked, "Are ye yet without understanding?" Another version translates that to "Are you still so dull?" Clearly, Jesus wanted them to widen their understandings, to open their ears and eyes to see and hear beyond the words, and to look again.

Spiritual Blindness

I often wonder why the gospel writers gave voice to their own blindness. They could have puffed themselves up, bragging about their insightful understandings from the start. Instead, they chose to show themselves as partially blind. It was not until the resurrection that their eyes fully opened and they understood Christ's message. What were they saying to us? To me? Are my eyes opened to what I need to see?

Eternal Light

I remember my dad's last few minutes on this earth. We were told that his departure from this earth could come at any time. We were gathered around his bed—my brother, my daughter, his dear friend Rosalie, and me. We were speaking with him, softly, placing ice chips on his parched lips. His eyes were closed now. We hung on his slow, labored breaths.

Gently, we gave him permission to go. I told him his brothers were waiting for him. His breathing slowed to a labored rattle. In the distance a harpist was playing "Time to Say Goodbye." Tears flowed. We braced for the end.

Then suddenly something changed. Unexpectedly his eyes opened. That almost never happened because one eyelid was always shut. Yet now both eyes were wide open. His gray complexion was now animated and bathed in light, as though an inner flame was ignited. We witnessed this new light and his transformation. With both eyes wide open, he went home.

The Second Light Rule: Look Again and Linger There

My dad's eyes opened to the eternal flame. With new light, he saw, and he understood. But I am tethered to earthly eyes that may not always see. I imagined Jesus, as he reprimanded his disciples, saying lovingly to me, "Gloria, my child, why are you so dull?"

> Now lift up your eyes and look from the
> place where you are, northward and southward
> and eastward and westward. (Gen. 13:14)

The Second Light Rule is simply this: to look beyond the mundane; to look beyond what we do not understand; to look beyond our petty grievances, our differences, our knee-jerk reactions, our fears, our groupness, and our worries; to see what is in plain sight. Connections. Flame. Everywhere. In all directions.

Second Light allows us to really see goodness that we might readily dismiss—things we see yet unsee. Our neighbor helping us lift a heavy package. A giggling child. A flower. A driver allowing us the right of way. A smile from a stranger when you need it. A teacher who really saw us. Butterflies.

Light a lamp to goodness. Spiritual light. Our God-sense. It is our backup light when we go through life's storms. It is there for the asking.

> Open my eyes so that I can see all the wonderful things in your teachings. (Ps. 119:18)

IN "PLANE" SIGHT

There is geometry in the humming of the strings,
there is music in the spacing of the spheres and
there is geometry in each arc of a flower.

—Pythagoras

Geometry draws the soul toward truth.
(Plato)

There was a time when I lived in the shadows of doubt. Did God exist? But Plato was right. It was geometry that drew me in. It made beautiful sense to me. Can anyone observe nature and not be enthralled with the spirals, the fractals, and the hand that designed it all?

In one of Christmas letters to my grandchildren, I gifted these thoughts to them: Your life will be surrounded by music, math, and design. I offer you these thoughts as you learn about them and as you inch toward truths in your life.

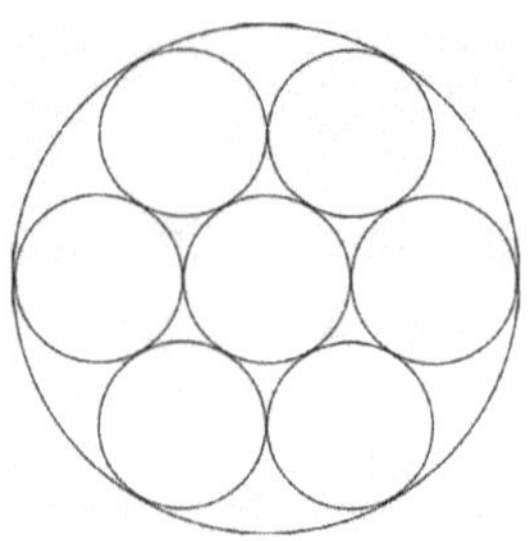

Circles

You are born within a wonderful circle of family and friends. As you grow, life takes on new risks. Your circle will expand. You will need guidance and wisdom to determine whom or what you allow inside.

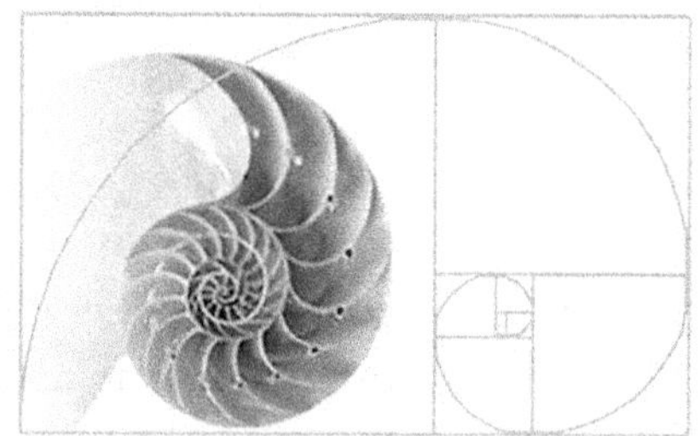

Rectangles and Squares (the Golden Ratio)

Four ninety-degree angles formed by two sets of parallel lines. Each corner represents structures of integrity: honesty, hard work, humor, and humility. As strong as they are, they can lean, become rhombic, and go askew. You will be tested. Be sure to have family and friends in your circle to keep you upright.

Triangles

Only three angles and three sides? Did we lose a side? You will face loss, and the question is, How will you deal with loss? We ache. We grieve. But know this: the triangle is the strongest of polygons. Strength can be born from loss.

Parallel Lines

These lines are equidistant and consistently follow each other. I will be your parallel line, following in your every move. Parallel lines supposedly never meet. Yet astrophysicists say that in the arc of the universe, on another sphere, they eventually meet.

When I cross over, remember, we will meet again.

Planes

Invisible boundaries are part of our lives. Planes are porous and often hard to see, which makes them so tempting and easy to cross. If you slip into a dangerous zone, we will welcome you back. If you lose your way, we will cross that plane to rescue you back. I know this because I have been rescued.

> The heavens declare the glory of God; and
> the firmament shows his handiwork. (Ps. 19:1)

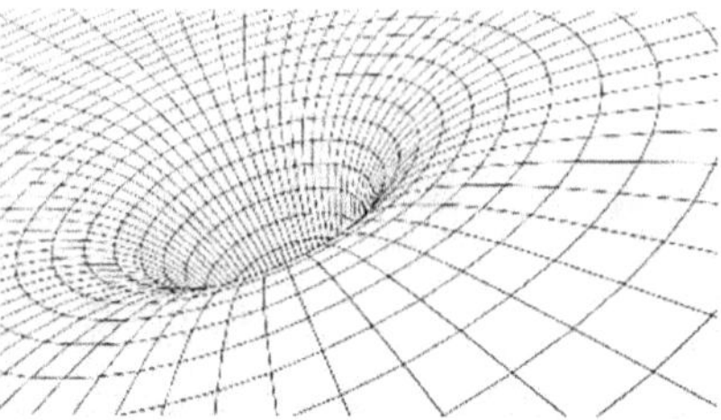

ARRIVING IN THE UNEXPECTED 

If you are faithful in little things, you will be faithful in large ones.
—Luke 16:10

In my quiet December courtyard, this festive maple tree was a feast for the eyes. People walking by would stop and wonder how this tree kept its colorful red leaves long into winter. Like a Christmas garland, it fit right in the holiday spirit. The bright crimson leaves created a holiday canopy for my outdoor winter nook. When the leaves fluttered, it looked like cardinals in flight.

But a sudden shift rearranged my world.

A northeaster blustered through my neighborhood. It rattled the doors and windows and sent trash cans rolling down the street. Hours later, when the storm finally relented, I looked outside and saw that my beautiful red maple was stripped bare.

Sudden Loss

I was unprepared for this sudden loss and equally unprepared for my reaction. The wind that tore at my tree also robbed something from me. It was another year of COVID, still distancing, still grieving losses.

The empty tree mirrored my own isolation. It took away all my pretenses for coping with COVID. It erased any sense of proportion. Laid bare was the grief and sorrow that I had kept tamped down. Maybe it hurt too much to acknowledge the unfathomable pain felt by those who lost jobs and loved ones. But now, I felt as naked as my tree. Sadness settled in. And I wore it like a thick overcoat, depressing my energy, depressing joy. I remained indoors. Head down. No walks.

The sorrow of the world rested heavily on my shoulders. But I was about to see there was more to the story.

Still Here but Differently…

Feeling the need to shake out of despair, I tentatively ventured outside. And wow! There was something so unexpected. My eyes rested on a beautiful carpet of red.

My leaves seemed to say, "Hey, I'm still here, only differently."

Like the thousands of lost souls gone from sight but exist in another plane, their spirit is here but differently. My mind leapt to a higher energy and danced in the thought.

Nature literally rolled out her red carpet for me. I know it may sound insignificant, even ridiculous, but this rearrangement of thought brought me back from despair. I wasn't prepared for this joy, but I felt the impulse to be faithful to it. And I remembered this verse from Luke:

> If you are faithful in the little things, you
> will be faithful in the large ones. (Luke 16:10)

The Late Harvest

More onion than early peas, layers upon layers, we are the late harvest.

HEARTS: NO EXPIRATION DATE

I know how bad this sounds, but I used to dread Mother's Day. I cringe even typing the words. But listen to my story.

My mother devoted her life to her four children. If she had any longings to be something else, to do something outside the confines of the house, something of her own, she kept it to herself. She was 100 percent a mom and a wife. And I felt she should have had more.

Regrettably, each year when the daffodils were signaling the arrival of May, the same old feelings would emerge, dreading that Sunday in May, all because I felt inadequate. How could I offer a gift that matched her selfless sacrifice for me? I began to think of Mother's Day as my day of guilt.

Whatever gift I might find could never be enough. I would search the stores and always seemed to settle on a present that felt like a trinket. This sense of inadequacy was only in my mind. My mother loved everything I gave her, and that only increased my sense of guilt. More sacrifice. More denial of self. I wanted more for her, even if she did not want it for herself. It never occurred to me she was living the life she wanted.

It took me a lifetime to figure it out, but finally, I got it. Mother's Day was not about rescuing her and certainly not about the gifts. Maybe it was about something else.

Maybe it was time to share my heart.

Another Mother's Day was soon to arrive. Feeling the same old tug, I decided to write a letter. It went something like this:

> Mom, I am sorry, but you will not be getting a store-bought gift for Mother's Day this year. Instead, I want to tell you what is in my heart, what I have longed to say and never have. There are moments in my childhood that I will treasure forever, little moments, so small that it might surprise you how I elevate them in my memories. So here are a few:

- When we did the dishes together, you washed, and I dried. I would prattle on about my day, school, and my friends. And you patiently listened to me. You were the best listener, and because you listened, I felt loved.

- When we went clothes shopping, you taught me how to look for quality. There was a day when you showed me how to inspect the skirt seams to see if the patterns and plaids matched. You would remind me repeatedly that it is better to buy one good thing of quality rather than buying a lot of cheaper things. You were my teacher, and I learned from you. Once or twice, I strayed from that advice, buying things of less quality to get more. Then your voice would come through loud and clear: *you get what you pay for*.

- You understood so well that I had a fierce independence and hated to be told what to do. Not that I was a slacker, but I wanted to do household chores before it became a request. I liked the illusion that I was in charge. You saw that need in me to be self-sufficient and gave me space to say, "Mom, I'm going outside and see if the clothes on the line are dry." And sometimes, with a little sparkle in your eyes, you would muse about something that needed to be done, like *Hmm, I wonder if the tables need dusting*. (Hints were not requests.) Within a few minutes, with great purpose, I would announce, "The furniture needs dusting. Leave it to me."

- You understood my love of nature, to take long walks in the woods and to climb our willow tree, with genuine indulgence. With a chuckle, you would tell people, "If you can't find Gloria, go look in a tree."

- I felt so much pride, walking with you to church, dressed in our finest, belonging to each other.

Tentatively, I mailed the letter and wondered if I would get a response. I did. A flurry of hugs and kisses seemed to underscore the value of that letter. She was more demonstrative than I ever remembered. She scooped me up and lifted me up off my feet. We hugged.

It was the most important embrace of my life. I still can feel the touch of that validation.

Three months later, my mother was suddenly taken from us. But here is more validation. That letter is now months, years, and decades long. I keep adding to it. And I know she is there receiving its message. There is no expiration date on love. It is eternal.

There is always time to share the heart, even now.

AS OLD AS TIME

The Southern Magnolia: As Old as Time Itself

Steel Magnolia

Breathtaking,
Delicate beauty
Of creamy perfection
With roots running deep
In southern soil
A history almost
As old as time
And endurance
As tough as
Steel.
(Patricia Neely-Dorsey)

The Southern Magnolia: This gem has no equal.

Unlike ground-level flowers that giggle and flirt for attention, the solitary magnolia is perched up high, too sophisticated to be governed by the wind. With edges that blush pink, these white jewels adorn the evergreen branches, looking like ornaments placed by hand.

When the morning sun lifts from its lavender haze, it illuminates each flower to an iridescent porcelain. The full bloom is like an open hand, inviting me closer where I get a hint of fragrant lemony citrus. More than her unrivaled beauty, I sense there is the depth of discovery.

The southern magnolia is a symbol of enduring strength and longevity. With an intricate root system that deeply anchors her to the earth, this tree is one of the most successful of plants. She is an old soul, as old as time, native to a young earth, surviving eons of geological and environmental changes. Little wonder that the magnolia is an inspiration to poets and writers.

Steel Magnolias

A favorite movie of mine is *Steel Magnolias*. Adapted from a play by Robert Harling and based on true events, the story is about the lives of five unique women whose friendship grows into a deeply rooted tour de force. They lean on each other with an endurance as tough as steel. When faced with a tragic loss, they grieve, regroup, and find the strength to carry on, together.

A memorable line is spoken by the cantankerous but lovable Ouiser (short for Louisa), who insists that she is not crazy—she has just been in a bad mood for forty years! Ouiser's support system, her steel magnolias, will not allow her to sink into moody despair and self-pity. She learns to laugh at herself. Here in the time of COVID, in the land of distanced relationships, I have my Ouiser moments. And like her, I have my lovable network of empowered women, my steel magnolias. I lean on them for humor, comfort, wisdom, and strength. Distance does not separate us. Our lives are interwoven threads of the same story.

With Roots Running Deep: A System of Thick Relationships

Steel Magnolias is a sometimes light, sometimes dramatic narrative of a tight-knit community of friends. We see ourselves and our relationships mirrored in this story. In his bestseller, *The Second Mountain*, David Brooks describes *community* as "thick systems of relationships." We are social beings. Our need for connection is in our DNA. You might be as surprised as I was to learn that strong interconnected relationships also occur deep underground in the plant world.

The Wood-Wide Web

What I am about to explain boggles my mind. Eons before Google, Twitter, and Facebook, a complex system of communication traveling throughout the plant world evolved. Known as mycelium, this underground fungal network is affectionately referred to by botanists as the "wood-wide" web. Not unlike our friends in *Steel Magnolias*, when trouble brews, plants sense danger and they help each other.

Nature's 911 Call

When plants signal stress, their neighbors secrete substances that travel up from their roots to above-ground branches and leaves to ward off nibbling invaders. They can even create conditions that attract the natural enemies of the invaders. And if a tree limb is suddenly severed, scientists say that the *ouch* is transmitted to the network, resulting in nourishing minerals sent by the collective. This remarkable network is so interrelated that if we could peer down so deep below the ground upon which we walk, one plant system would be indistinguishable from the other.

This is nature's magnificent collective, an organic force, as old as life itself.

A History Almost as Old as Time

Life is interconnected and interdependent. We laugh, cry, and thrive together. Your story is my story. I think back to the time before we became a mobile society, when family and friends gathered around the kitchen table and told the old stories. Like the magnolia, a symbol of endurance, our stories sustained each other.

I think of the Bible stories told to me in my growing-up years. Parables spoken by Jesus delivered messages of mercy and love. The powerful simplicity of those stories steeled my heart, like the magnolia, welcoming me into the collective of souls and saints, like an open hand ungoverned by the winds.

To teach forgiveness: *Father, forgive them for they know not what they do.*

To teach mercy: *Let he who is without sin cast the first stone.*

To teach faith: *Ask, and the door will open.*

To teach about love: *Love one another as I have loved you.*

To give purpose: *Follow me. I will make you fishers of men.*

To teach compassion: *When you do it for the least of them, you do it for me.*

When asked whom my neighbor is, he tells the parable of the good Samaritan, a lowly person of undesirable culture and religion who becomes our model for compassion.

> We, being many, are one body in Christ,
> and individually, members one of another. (Rom.
> 12:5)

EQUINOX: BALANCE AND RECOVER

Equinox

Equal days, equal nights,
Winged geese taking flight.
Apples, plums, grapes, and pears
Harvested in waning light.

Equal warm, equal cold,
Leaves still clinging to their hold.
Blowing seeds, the winds of change
Seasons come and rearrange.

What to say, what goes forth,
Emotions high, south, and north.
Calming down, flow and flux
Balanced as the equinox.

Equal seasons come and go,
Rhythms strum the time to know.
So many seeds seeking root,
Ye shall know them by their fruit.

RISING FROM THE FOG

Overnight, the Atlantic Ocean rolled out a silent blue-gray mist. It hovered over coastal inlets and drifted through the trees behind my house before spilling onto the street. From my window I saw a world wrapped in puffy cotton balls and I was as excited as a child waking up to winter's first snow. There is nothing more soothing or more mysterious than a walk in the fog. It was what I needed.

Stepping into the gauzy mist, I took in a lungful. Swallowed up in quiet dream clouds, I felt shielded from the sorrows, tragedies, and injustices of the world. Van Morrison depicted fog as illusion and confusion that hangs heavily over the world, menacingly foreboding. But for me, it is a soft, insulating portal, inviting me to enter.

So I continue my walk with the belief that something beautiful might be unveiled. Mysteries tend to linger in places like fog, waiting to be discovered.

Mysteries in the Lifting

Comfort cushioned me in the mist. Poet Carl Sandburg compared fog to a stealth cat, sneaking in on little cat feet. I see fog as a velvet glove with outspread fingers, pointing me into places unknown. Like clouds, fog is a collection of tiny water droplets. And water, the source of life, is also the stuff of tears. This morning I was held in the soft palm of this apparition, searching for clarity.

The pond behind my house was coming into view, untouched by the fog, appearing clear and pristine. There under a canopy of gray, it presented itself like the mystical Brigadoon, rising from its hundred-year sleep. Something inside of me stirred. *Am I also awakening from slumber?* No answers came. Sometimes it is enough to wonder.

A family of ducks floated effortlessly on the pond's glassy surface. I imagined myself floating downstream with them, drifting me away from all the risk—reward COVID decisions I would be making, amid all the pain, sadness, injustices, and tragedies in our world. The complacency of the pond was a pleasant escape…but only momentarily.

I found myself clinging to the story of Brigadoon, clear, bright, and rising from the mist. Is it a metaphor for humankind? Do the generations advance day by day, year by year? Or does it take a hundred-year event, something once hidden and now visible, to awaken us from our slumber?

Purpose

Life has purpose. My life has purpose. I am here to heal and love, even when it is not easy and maybe especially when it is not easy. But I do not wander aimlessly in a fog of despair, under shrouds of uncertainty searching for lighted pathways. I was given a model, whose life here on earth showed me how to live, how to forgive, and how to love.

This is my clarity in the morning fog: tomorrow's story starts today with me. With resolve. In rivulets of goodwill for all humankind. If my purpose is cloudy or unclear, I must look for the gloved signs, pointing the way.

TENDING MY GARDEN WITHIN:
THE POWER OF ONE

My pot of impatiens
Lovely and quiet.
I wonder why it
Prefers the private
Shelter of shade.

When asked she conveyed,
Self-assured and unafraid,
I'm happy for grand
Blooms in the sun.

But do not downgrade
A place in the shade.
To understand
The power of one.

We've all been kissed
With incredible gifts,
That honor and build
A life that's been given…
A life worth living.

ABOUT THE AUTHOR

Whether hiking in the Vail Valley, beautiful Lake Arrowhead, the lush pinelands of Southern New Jersey, or walking under the swaying palms of central Florida, I comingle with nature—mind, body, and soul.

Thomas Merton said it best: *"The sky is my prayer, the birds are my prayer, the wind in the trees is my prayer, for God is in all things."*

The early morning hours ignite my God-sense. The earth awakens to a chorus of birdsong that pierce and polish the dawn. Layers of blues, purples, and pinks give hint to a burst of sunrise. I ease into soft spaces where human drama cannot exist. A groundswell of gratitude renders me weightless. Unaccompanied yet not alone, I hear:

And lo, I am with you always.

Check out Gloria's Blog: https://gloriasstories.com